THE TRUE-OR-FALSE BOOK OF
DOGS

by **Patricia Lauber**

Illustrated by **Rosalyn Schanzer**

HarperCollins*Publishers*

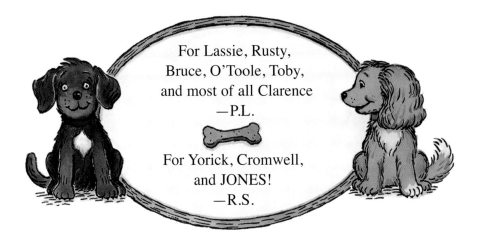

For Lassie, Rusty,
Bruce, O'Toole, Toby,
and most of all Clarence
—P.L.

For Yorick, Cromwell,
and JONES!
—R.S.

The True-or-False Book of Dogs
Text copyright © 2003 by Patricia Lauber
Illustrations copyright © 2003 by Rosalyn Schanzer
Manufactured in China. All rights reserved.
www.harperchildrens.com

Library of Congress Cataloging-in-Publication Data
Lauber, Patricia.
The true-or-false book of dogs /by Patricia Lauber ; illustrated by Rosalyn Schanzer.
p.   cm.
ISBN 0-06-029767-0 — ISBN 0-06-029768-9 (lib. bdg.)
1. Dogs—Miscellanea—Juvenile literature.   I. Schanzer, Rosalyn.   II. Title.
SF426.5 .L43   2003   636.7—dc21   2001051911

1 2 3 4 5 6 7 8 9 10
❖
First Edition

Dogs on title page: Afghan hound (left) and smooth-haired dachshund (right)
Dogs on copyright page and contents page: mixed-breed puppies

CONTENTS

DOGS AND PEOPLE

The story of dogs and people begins long ago, at a time when there were no dogs, only wolves. People of that time moved about in bands, camping where they found food and water. Wolves lived in the same areas, and in ways the two groups were alike. Wolves also lived in bands, or packs. They hunted the same prey and drank from the same streams and lakes. People often worked together when hunting. So did wolves. Also, each group feared the other.

At some time wolves learned that where there were people there might be food. When people made a big kill, they took the animal parts they wanted and left the rest. Wolves and other animals ate it. Near their camps, people had dumps where they threw bones, fish heads, and other food garbage. Wolves found food in the dumps.

Some wolves began to follow the hunters and to hang around camps. At night the people gathered within the circle of firelight, for the dark held many terrors. The camp wolves gathered just outside, in the shadows.

At first people must have feared the wolves and tried to drive them away. The wolves came slinking back. In time people became used to them. The bolder wolves came closer. Because people like to feed animals, these people probably threw bits of food to the friendlier wolves. They slept better at night, because the wolves kept guard and barked or growled if other animals came near.

The camp wolves came to think of the people as their pack. They defended their pack and their territory against other wolves. They no longer mixed and mated with outside wolves, only with other camp wolves.

The camp wolves changed. On the outside they still looked exactly like wolves. But inside they were different. They had lost their fear of people. Camp wolves were friendly and social. They were guards. They may have helped human hunters—tracking and herding prey. They were loyal to their human pack. They had become dogs.

Scientists say that the first dogs appeared about 135,000 years ago. For thousands of years they went on looking like wolves. But they had chosen to live with people. The long friendship between people and dogs had begun.

Read on and see how much you know about our friend the dog.

Only some dogs are descended from wolves

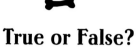

True or False?

Look at a St. Bernard, a French poodle, and a chihuahua. It's hard to believe that they are all the same kind of animal. It's even harder to believe that they are all descended from wolves. And that is why scientists used to think dogs must have other ancestors as well. Now today's scientists have proved that idea is wrong. All dogs are descended from wolves and only from wolves.

St. Bernard   chihuahua   French poodle

GREY WOLF   CHINESE WOLF   INDIAN WOLF

The wolves varied in size, color, and behavior. That is, they had different traits, and so the first dogs did too.

When groups of early people met, they often exchanged gifts and traded dogs. That is how different traits spread from one area to another.

Sometimes a litter had a pup or two with a new trait—perhaps a gray coat with big patches of white. People liked that trait. They could tell at a glance whether an animal was a dog or a wolf. They liked other traits they saw from time to time—smaller jaws and teeth, rounder eyes, lop ears, a curly tail. They mated dogs that had these traits with other dogs that also had them. And so the traits were passed on. When this happened, dogs no longer looked just like wolves. They probably looked much like the dingo of Australia. And they went on looking that way for hundreds of years.

dingo

Dogs changed when human lives changed

True or False?

Dogs looked the same for hundreds of years because for hundreds of years they had only two main jobs. They guarded the camp and they helped hunters. Dogs had all the hunting skills of wolves. They could track prey, drive it into ambush, bring it down, or hold it in place for the hunters to kill.

Dogs changed only when human ways of life changed — when people started to farm, settle down, and build towns. Now there were more jobs for dogs to do.

GUARD DOG

SHEEPHERDING DOG

Property had to be guarded. Big fierce dogs were wanted.

Farm animals were being raised for meat and hides. Dogs kept the animals from wandering and protected them from wolves and big cats. For this job a dog with a coat of several colors was needed, a dog that could be easily told from a wolf.

Townspeople and farmers were troubled by rats and other small pests. They needed a small dog that could hunt prey in small places, such as burrows. They bred for size just the way they had bred for curly tails, by mating the runts of litters over and over again.

Before long there were hunting dogs, sheepdogs, farm dogs, war dogs, companion dogs, guard dogs, and pets that were small enough to pick up and carry around.

FARM DOG

PET DOG

The ancient Egyptians had cats but not dogs

True or False?

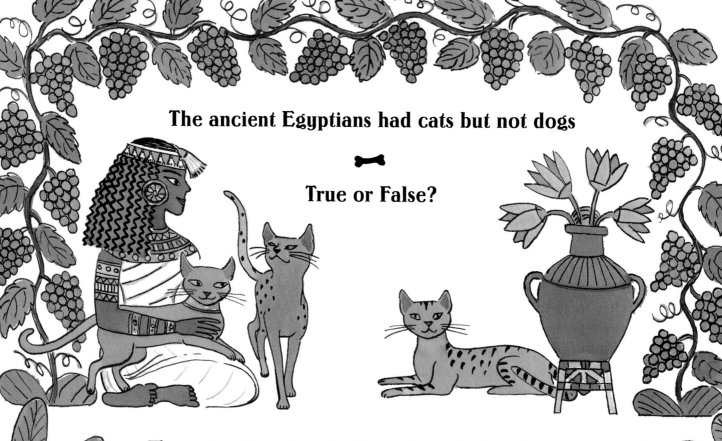

The ancient Egyptians had lots of cats. In fact, they were probably the first people in the world to have tame cats. But they also had several kinds of dog, which appear in their art. One was a special hunting dog.

Egypt was a land of wide-open spaces. Hunters wanted a dog that could see prey in the distance, chase it, and run it down. Five thousand years ago, they bred a dog with a slender body and long legs that hunted mostly by sight. We call this kind of dog a sight hound. Today the most famous sight hound is the greyhound, which can run as fast as 40 miles an hour.

pharaoh hound

molossus

Other ancient peoples also had specially bred dogs. The Greeks and the Romans liked white sheepdogs because they blended in with the sheep. The Romans had a big dog, which they called the molossus. It was used to guard property, pull carts, and attack enemy troops. They also had sight hounds. They had hounds that hunted by scent. And they had small dogs that were pets.

Chinese lapdog

Two or three thousand years ago, the Chinese were breeding dogs for hunting, guarding, and eating. They also had a small, short-legged, flat-faced dog that was a pet and lapdog. It may have been an ancestor of today's Pekingese.

turnspit

Most breeds of dogs are fairly new

🦴

True or False?

Soldier, sailor, explorer, trader—they all brought dogs home from distant lands. Even so, a thousand years ago western Europe probably had only a dozen types of dog. Each was bred to do certain work. Dogs that did the same work looked somewhat alike.

A book published in 1570 names seventeen breeds, among them terrier, bloodhound, sight hound, setter, spaniel, mastiff, sheepdog, turnspit. A turnspit worked in the kitchen, turning the spit that held a roast over a fire.

By 1850 another book named forty breeds.

A dog show in 1890 had more than two hundred classes.

The big jump in numbers was caused by a big change in the way people lived in Europe and North America. Inventions of the 1800s led to the building of factories and mills. People from farms and villages flocked to towns and cities, seeking work.

Many people no longer needed working dogs. But they liked dogs and wanted dogs. They started having contests for best dogs and breeding new kinds. The contests led to setting standards for how breeds should look—how, for example, the head should be shaped. At shows dogs were judged for looks.

There are now three or four hundred breeds—no one is sure of the exact number.

pomeranian   harrier   deerhound

15

A dog treats a bone the way
a wolf treats extra food

🦴

True or False?

When wolves kill a large deer, they may have more meat than they can eat at a sitting. To save it and hide it from other animals, they tear off big chunks and bury them.

While holding a chunk in its jaws, a wolf digs a hole with its front feet. It drops the meat into the hole and uses its nose to fill the hole with loose dirt. Returning later, the wolf digs up the meat, shakes off the dirt, and settles down to eat.

Most dogs do not bury food to save it. They can't. Pet food is not made to be picked up, carried, and buried. A big bone is different. It is easy to carry. It can be chewed on and enjoyed, but it cannot be eaten up. It is left over. And so a dog does with it what a wolf does with leftovers — buries the bone, using its nose to fill in the hole.

mixed breed ▶

16

Dogs hear more than we do

🦴

True or False?

If sounds are low pitched, dogs hear just about what humans do. But at higher pitches they hear far more. Like wolves, they hear sounds that we don't hear at all, such as the squeals of mice and rats.

Wolves are able to hear a howl from four miles away. Dogs also hear sounds too faint for our ears. They hear the family car arriving long before we hear a car door slam. They know the footsteps of a family member and are at the door to say, "Welcome!" before the key touches the lock.

Dogs and wolves have the same sense of smell

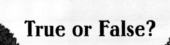

True or False?

Wind may carry the scent of a deer to wolves that are a mile away. Within moments the hunt is on.

    Dogs have inherited the same keen sense of smell. They use their noses to find mates, tell friend from foe, hunt, find their way home, track.

bloodhound

A trained dog can pick up a scent from the ground and track it for miles. If the scent is fresh, it can even tell which way the person or animal was heading. A newer step has a tiny bit more odor than an older one.

Most things give off odors. The odors take the form of gases that mix with the air. When you breathe air through your nose, the gases are moistened. Nerve cells sense them. The nerve cells send messages to your brain, and that is when you smell the odor.

A dog's nose works the same way yours does. But a dog has 220 million smell-sensing cells, while a human has only 5 million. And that is why dogs can smell all sorts of things that we can't. Dogs live in a world of smells that we cannot even imagine. In that world they somehow manage to pick out the odors that are of interest and to shut out the others.

◀ **pointer**

Dogs see what we see

▬

True or False?

Dogs have good eyesight, but they do not see exactly what we see. They are, for example, quick to see movement, but they do not see much detail.

Like human eyes, dog eyes have two kinds of cells that sense light. Cone cells sense color and are useful only in bright light. Rod cells sense black, white, and gray, and are useful for seeing in dim light. Humans and dogs see when light enters the eye and falls on these cells, which send messages to the brain.

Human eyes see all the colors of the rainbow. Dogs see some color, but they cannot see anything like the range of colors that we do. In dim light, though, they see much better. One reason is that a dog's eyes have special cells that act like mirrors. They gather up light that escaped the other cells and bounce it back into the eye. A dog uses every bit of light that enters its eyes.

What a dog does and doesn't see is what its wolf ancestors did and didn't see. Wolves usually hunt at dawn and at dusk. They don't need to see color. They need to see well in dim light. They don't need to see detail. They need to see movement—the fleeing prey.

Dogs bark less than wolves do

True or False?

A dog's barking comes in bursts of short, sharp sounds. Dogs bark when they're hungry, when they want to go out, when they want to come in, when they can't reach their toy, when their owner comes home.

Barking often warns the human pack that someone is coming. A barking dog is usually not intending to bite. It is sounding the alarm. Barking may go on for a long time, until the cause goes away or humans come to find out what's happening. Sometimes dogs bark and bark for no reason that humans can see.

Dogs bark much more than wolves do. Wolves do bark, but they don't have much need to. They don't bark often. They don't keep it up. And they bark more softly. A wolf is most likely to bark when it sees something strange and is not sure what to do. The bark tells the stranger, "I've seen you." It also alerts the rest of the pack.

Early humans bred dogs for barking, just as they did for curved tails. Noisy barkers made better guards.

komondor (outside)
Irish setter (inside)▶

French hound

Dogs howl more than wolves do

🦴

True or False?

Wolves howl to call the pack together. The howling says, "We are here. Join us!" Wolves howl most often when they are ready to go hunting.

Most dogs are part of a human pack. They have no need to call their pack together and go hunting. When mealtime comes, a human puts down a bowl of food. Dogs do not howl nearly as often as wolves do.

When a dog does howl, it is usually lonely—shut up by itself or left behind when its humans went off for the day. But the howl means just what a wolf's howl does: "I am here. Join me!"

Some dogs howl when their humans are singing. They seem to think their pack is howling, and so they throw back their heads and join in.

A dog's body may tell of its feelings

True or False?

Dogs and wolves cannot talk in words, but they can say a lot with their bodies. One dog can make its feelings clear to another.

Australian silky terrier

bulldog

doberman

Dogs have senses that humans don't

True or False?

mixed breed

Dogs sense things that humans don't. The reason is often that their senses of hearing and smell are much keener than ours.

When dogs sense a thunderstorm before we do, they seem to have an extra sense. But they are really using their sense of hearing.

Like cats and horses, dogs may become upset hours before an earthquake takes place. Scientists think they are hearing noises from the earth that we cannot hear.

Sometimes a dog freezes in place. It stares, although a human can see nothing. Fur rises along its back. It growls. Then suddenly the dog goes back to normal. Owners sometimes say their dog has seen a ghost. More likely, the dog's keen nose has picked up the strong scent of some strange animal.

mixed breed

But dogs do have other senses that humans don't have. They can find their way home from far away. They are guided in some way by the earth's magnetic field, but no one knows how. Cats and other animals have this same sense. If humans ever had this sense, we have lost it.

St. Bernards and other big dogs may be used to hunt for humans buried by avalanches. Rescuers have long said that the dogs can sense whether the victim is still alive by sniffing the snow. Scientists think they can now explain how the dogs do this. At least some breeds, they say, have special cells in their noses that can detect body heat.

St. Bernard

Today pet dogs outnumber working dogs

True or False?

golden retriever

beagle

Today some 55 million dogs live in the United States alone, some of them purebreds and some mixed breeds, or mutts. Many are still valued workers. They do their old jobs of hunting, herding, and guarding. They do new jobs of tracking and of sniffing out drugs and explosives. They also guide the blind, visit and cheer the elderly and the sick, act in movies.

But most dogs are companions and pets—friends. They are playful if we want to play, loving when we are lonely or sad, always there when we want company. And even the tiniest lapdog is as brave as a wolf when it comes to defending its human pack.

German shepherd

mixed breed